Praise for
To Be Soul, Do
In Creative Consciousness.

"*To Be Soul, Do Soul* is a glowing leaping catalyst and buoyant companion for transformation from the inside that results in changes on the outside. Hiro is a seer and sayer for this world and all the other dimensions."
SARK, Bestselling author, artist and speaker

"This is not a self-help tome or a how-to be better guide or something that can be apprehended in a rush. For, this book you hold? It is a return home. A call to Presence. A call to remember the love which you crave and search for and yet are never separate from."
Jennifer Louden, Best-selling author, teacher

"This truly stunning book has changed my life. The evocative and profound invitations in this book continue to be a guided journey back to my Self. When I'm struggling, I pick up the book and the author seems to be speaking directly to me, helping me transmute the negativity of the situation I'm experiencing and reminding me of my divine radiance."
Maia Caron, Author of *Song of Batoche*

"Hiro Boga's newest book knows us well. With a gentle, wise and playful spirit, it offers ways for us to leave behind – if only for a moment, or a moment that may last forever – the distances with which we've learned to live our complicated, overburdened lives, so that we may return to the wholeness we have never left behind. Every page offers a pathway home."
Peter Levitt, Author of *Fingerpainting on the Moon: Writing & Creativity as a Path to Freedom*

"Hiro seamlessly weaves stillness and action, movement and meditation, inquiry and experimentation to remind us that we are all inherently beautiful, powerful, and whole, and that joy and integrity are byproducts of curiosity and the creative process."
Jena Schwartz, MFA, Writer, editor, teacher

Reaching for this book helps to slow my breathing, reconnect within and get back in tune."

Andrea J. Lee, Master Coach, CEO of Thought Partners International, Bestselling author and speaker.

"This is the best kind of book from one of my favorite thought leaders... it speaks poetically right to the entire being."

Michelle Wolff, Coach, Creator of the *Sovereign Storytellers Podcast*

"Beautiful daily practices to get in touch with your inner guidance."

Mal Duane, Author of *Alpha Chick: Five Steps for Moving from Pain to Power*

"The practices are easy to do and don't take much time. But they are powerful."

Theresa Reed, Author of *The Tarot Colouring Book.*

"...a soothing, searing elixir that takes all of the rough edges in your world and gently, purposefully smooths them into true works of art. You will not be the same, the world cannot be the same, when you make the choice to bring these ideas alive."

Lisa Murray, Author of *Living Beyond Burnout*

"This powerful book lives up to its subtitle, *Adventures in Creative Consciousness*. It has the ingredients to change not only your life, but the world..."

Margaret Schwartz

"Each page provides prompts for deep reflection and heightened awareness. With each page, I felt my connection to my soul becoming more and more firm."

Michele T. Woodward, Executive Coach, Author of eight books

"[A book] that can easily be picked up at any time and find nourishment for the soul."

Cassie Jeans, Author of *Her Art of Surrender*

TO BE SOUL, DO SOUL

Adventures in Creative Consciousness

TO BE SOUL DO SOUL

Adventures in Creative Consciousness

HIRO BOGA

DEVA PUBLISHING
LANTZVILLE • BC • CANADA

Cover and interior design: Calyx Design

Published by Deva Publishing, P.O. Box 94
Lantzville, BC V0R 2H0 Canada

HiroBoga.com

PREFACE

Lay down any agenda you have for this book. If you've picked this volume up with a desire to be better or different than you are, or if the tick-tock of the modern world is so loud in your ears you have in mind just a quick scan of these pages, I believe I can hear the "neglected presence" of your soul chuckling – to quote John O'Donohue, whose works remind me of Hiro's. This is not a self-help tome or a how-to be better guide or something that can be apprehended in a rush. For, this book you hold? It is a return home. A call to Presence. Yours, of course, and Presence with a capital P. A call to remember the love which you crave and search for and yet are never separate from.

Roll these words around on the tongue of your heart. Avoid gulping. Let what you recognize here seep in through the cracks where the light gets in. We all have so many cracks and isn't that good news! Well, at least it is today.

While you are at it, abandon the tick-tock, the get-it-done anxiety that might be pinging away in the back of your mind, the ticklish urge to figure this life of yours out now, once and for all. Make like water and pool, with Hiro's guidance sinking like warm pebbles into your deliciously muddy depths.

How is it that someone comes to understand such mysteries, to understand what it means to be human, to know exactly how to help us stand on our own two feet proudly and look out at the world with the eyes of Love? How is it that person then hones the skills necessary to translate all these insights into instructions that illuminate our path home to our own hearts so clearly? Heck if I know. All I know is, how fortunate we are. How fortunate I am. It is a rare and beautiful thing indeed, what we have here. I will pour it over my parched heart for many years to come.

To be immersed in this world is to feel, to glimpse, and even to "grok" the vastness that exceeds you and animates you. You will turn these pages and be altered by yet again recognizing that you already have inside you all that you have been waiting for.

Thank you Hiro for opening our eyes to our own treasures.

– *Jennifer Louden*

AUTHOR'S NOTE

You are an incarnate, embodied soul. You don't have to *do* anything to be soul – soul is who you are. But you experience the depth, beauty, power and radiance of your soul's presence when you embody and express it in your everyday life.

Bring your soul into every moment of your life by doing what soul does. To be soul, do soul.

Be kind. Be generous. Be loving. Be powerful.

Be discerning, tender, playful, creative.

Bless the people and places you encounter each day. Bless yourself, your beloveds, your creations, your world. Partner with the Devas of your home and neighbourhood, your country, humanity, other beings who share this planet with you, and the Earth herself, to serve the perfect unfolding of the lives in their care.

Embrace all of who you are – your infinite, unbounded, universal beingness, and your quirky, unique, particular personhood. Your thoughts and feelings, your shadows and radiance, the golden threads of your desires, the silver threads of your passions.

Wholeness is the landscape of your soul.

The more you act from your soul-self, the more you will strengthen your inner radiance and become a source of soul in your world.

It's a simple enough practice. Set a timer on your phone to chime each hour, or four times a day, or as often as you wish. When it chimes, stop whatever you're doing. Take a moment to check in with yourself.

Where is your consciousness, in relationship to your body? Are you in your head? Your belly? Your right big toe? Are you miles away? Hovering someplace in the vicinity of, but not actually present in your body?

Take your awareness a foot or so up above the top of your head, and drop straight down from there into the center of your head. Behind your eyes and up a bit.

Expand the light of your awareness to fill the whole of your head. Staying centered in the center of your head, let your awareness radiate from there down through your neck and shoulders, your arms and hands, into your chest and heart, your diaphragm and belly, your spine and back, your pelvis and hips, your legs, ankles and feet.

With practice, this will only take a moment.

Now, notice where your soul is, in relationship to you. Is it behind you? Above you? Off to one side? Hanging out someplace in the stratosphere?

Turn to face your soul, and move towards it. Embrace it with all the desire and need with which you take in your next breath. Be one with your soul. Feel what happens when you blend with your soul fully and completely.

Return to whatever it is you were doing when your timer chimed its reminder. How do you experience the task at hand now, from this place of embodied soul?

To Be Soul, Do Soul is a collection of mini-experiments in energy and consciousness – ways to play with and explore the depth and breadth of your soul's reach, understand the boundaries and potentials of its expression in your life, and grow your capacity to be a source of soul in the world.

These experiments are portals, entryways into the vastness of your own soul, and into the multidimensional realms of consciousness as they intersect with everyday life here on earth.

There are no right or wrong ways to engage with these practices.

They are explorations, mini-adventures. Each one will lead you someplace that only you can go, in that moment. And each time you revisit them, you'll find yourself in the midst of a new adventure.

You can play with a new one each day, or work in greater depth with a single exploration for a week, or for however long you wish. You'll know how long to continue with a particular exploration by the juice, awe, simplicity or joy it holds for you.

When you get tired, or distracted, stop. Do something physical to ground yourself and your discoveries – go for a walk, or stretch, or climb a rock or hill, or take a hot bath. Whatever helps you reconnect with your body, and bring your soul's adventure into your physical world.

Approach these practices in a spirit of openness, curiosity and playful experimentation. Try them, and follow where they lead.

You may want to devote a journal to this practice, and write notes about your discoveries after each experiment. You may also want to create your own exploratory practices, as you become more familiar with the way this process works for you.

May they bring you joy, learning, delight, and adventure as you grow into a powerfully generative source of soul in your world.

Be a silken cocoon in a prickly-pear world.

✻

Be the feathery green of spring leaves. Let the winds of change lift you into a new dance.

❖

Be the & that links someone else's story with the world's story.

Be the murmur of underground streams, singing the soul home.

Cradle the world's grief tenderly; swaddle it in soul silk lullabies.

❋

Offer your beauty to the world.

Love all that is helpless, hopeless, lost or abandoned within you.
Without trying to fix or change it. Feel it. Love it.

*

Let the horizon kiss each footfall. Let Grace's clear vision illuminate every step you take.

Embrace the power of the creative No. What do you need to say a kind and loving No to, in order to feel whole, generative, joyful – and free to say Yes to what's calling you next? Say No to that.

✻

Surrender all that is painful, difficult, knotted, prickly or gnarled to the pattern that love holds for its perfect unfolding. Rest in the peace of holy surrender.

✣

Celebrate whatever is happening in this moment. It holds the entire miracle of your life.

Whether this moment holds joy or sorrow or both, numbness or exquisite communion or the rigours of justice meted or denied, it is the portal through which you enter the great mystery of who you are and why you're here.

Mother yourself. Mother your beloveds. Mother your creations. Mother your world.

Know yourself mothered. By your ancestors and lineage. By the soul of the earth and the soul of the cosmos. By the circle of your beloveds. By the Great Mother of all beings. By all who love you. By all who are invested in the success of your incarnation.

Rest in the womb of the world. Be the womb of the world.

Speak your truth, kindly, fiercely, clearly. Without equivocation. Unattached to outcome. Speak it because the body of truth is sacred. It needs no veiling or adornment. It simply is.

✻

Be patient with all that is seeking its rightful place within you. Hold tenderly, in a spacious heart, those filaments of light and shadow that weave new patterns from which your future, and the future of our world, will emerge. Matrix weaving happens in its own, sacred timing.

✵

See that threshold? It's here, now. Step over it. Don't hesitate. Don't look back. One step, and you're on the other side.

You've brought all of yourself into this new landscape. Breathe its lavender air.

Do the birds sing in a major key here? The sun still rises in the East. It still turns your cheek to gold.

What is the same, here? What is different? Who are you becoming, in the space between?

※

Move through the day with the directness of a two-year-old. Feel what you feel. Want what you want. Love what you love.

Take the simplest route from here to there. Stop for a nap, a snack, a hug, or a wandering bug. Stomp, dance, splash, twirl – do whatever your heart desires.

Be your desire in action.

Find the movement of joy in your body. Whether joy is a river in full flood, or the tiniest, almost imperceptible breath, it is yours; it is in you. Feel it.

Now, within this movement of joy in your body, feel the pattern of joy that your soul holds for you. Hold it in a spacious, open heart. Invite it to expand your capacity to hold, experience, express joy.

Be the field of joy.

How does your joy want to offer itself to your world? Do that. Lift someone up. Sing. Dance, twirl, write, play, make art. Give joy a shape, a form. Serve it in a silver bowl.

That loose thread in the fabric of your life, in the fabric of your business – the one that snags on your fingernail time and time again? That action you've known you needed to take, but haven't yet taken – because it feels daunting, uncomfortable, so you put it off for another day? Act on that today.

Take all the crash and roar, all the insistent noise in and around you, and put it in a big-bellied jar. Seal it with a tightly fitted lid. Place it in a corner of your room.

Experience the silence and simplicity of your own mind – free of worry, free of opinions, judgments, agendas, to-do lists. Float on the sea of spaciousness.

Float until the current of life bumps you gently onto this shore or that. Explore where you've landed. Follow the trail that calls you.

❄

If you cannot digest it, let it go. No matter how shiny and gorgeous, how lusciously tempting it might be, if you cannot digest it, it will poison you.

Whatever you've ingested, or are about to ingest, meet it with curiosity and discernment. Release it with love. Liberate yourself from anything that doesn't belong with you.

When you can no longer bear the unbearable, lie face-down on the ground. Yield all of you – your sorrow and pain; your yearning heart; your tormented body-mind; your radiant soul whose light you can no longer see – to the healing balm of the Sacred.

Feel yourself held in an embrace unfathomably vast, powerful, loving – and as tender as a mother with her newborn.

Rest. Rest. Let That which bears you, hold, reveal and bless you. Let the miracle enfold you.

Relinquish the urge to wrestle the world around you into the shape of your expectations. There are no narratives that will fit your perfectly square holes.

Let the stories you meet today show you their freckles, the miracles hidden under that unruly thatch of hair, within their glistening folds.

Be curious. What wonders reveal themselves when you let your expectations dissolve, when you take down the barriers between you and your world?

Life offers itself to you today, in all its briny beauty. Taste its salt on your mouth; let it linger on your tongue. Let it alchemize the elemental you – lead to gold.

Seal your senses. Anoint your ears, your eyelids, your mouth, your skin, your nostrils with the oil of seclusion.

Enter the sanctuary of your belly, your heart. Feel your soul's silken skin under your fingertips; warm yourself at the hearth of wholeness, at the fires of belonging.

Bring back the nectar of truth to renew your world.

Attune to the soul of Humanity, to the vision it holds for the evolution of our species. Why are we here? What is our role in the family of life on this earth?

Invite the pattern that the Deva of Humanity holds, in its energy field, into your own body, into your life.

What does it feel like, to be fully human? How does your embodied humanity embrace the multitude of other life-forms on our planet? What impact does a truly evolved humanity have, on our world?

Attune to our deep ancestors, who descended from the safety of treetops to the uncertain terrain of forest floor or savannah. They, who first walked upright 6 or 7 million years ago, didn't know what their actions would mean, for us, their daughters and sons who have arrived here all these millions of years later. They couldn't imagine what this shift to a vertical stance would mean for the history of the world.

To stand upright, to see the horizon eye-to-eye for the first time, when all you've ever known of the ground was a narrow negotiation between belly and grassland... Such courage! Such willingness to adventure in search of sustenance!

Where do these ancestors live, in your body? Get down on all fours and experience your world, for a few moments, from that horizontal stance. Belly low to the ground and protected. You are longer than you are tall. What do you know of the world around you? Which of your senses is keenest, most reliable in this horizontal orientation to your world?

Slowly, stand upright. Feel the shift in your body, in your primary modes of sensing and perception, in your relationship with the horizon, with your environment. Feel the flow of human evolution in the arches of your feet, in the way light enters your eyes.

Move through your day with the awareness that every choice you make today will reverberate through to your descendants. You are the activity of the Deva of Humanity. You are the ancestor of the generations to come. You are the blade of the knife that carves the shape of our world.

✳

Meet one of the looming, impossible-to-scale mountains within you. Meet it face-to-face. Notice its shape, its size, its adamant vertiginous topography. Place your hands and feet on its slippery, scree-lined slope. Notice the trackless paths you'd have to traverse to climb its granite body.

Feel its dangers: those scimitar rocks that can slice open an artery – the thin, unbreathable air that shivers at its peak. Feel the tremble and lurch, the cold despair the mountain's shadow casts on your heart, in your belly. Feel it.

Call your soul into this fragile communion. As its sun blazes through, all is illuminated: The mountain, your lurching heart, the space between you.

Notice your ferrous arms, your powerful, unyielding legs. Breathe in the sky of your own levitation.

Discern the true shape of the mountain before you. Feel its curves in the swivel of your hips, its caves in the secret passages of your body.

Know yourself, the mountain. Know the mountain, yourself. Touch of fingertip on lip. Intimate mystery.

Practice the art of choosing.

Invite your entire to-do / wish-I-could-do list to a party. Embrace each guest who arrives at your front door. Hang up their coats. Offer them glasses of champagne, just-picked raspberries, platters heaped with delectable confections. Introduce them to each other.

Bathe in the burble of their delight, the zing and fizz of cross-pollination. Which of your guests do you want to take by the hand? Sit down with, in a quiet corner of the garden, for deeper conversation?

Which ones move you, entice your curiosity, enliven your senses? Which ones enfold you in the musk of their skin, in the irresistible tide of their presence?

Choose those.

※

Be the honey in someone else's tea.

Be the fire that cooks someone else's stew, the oven that bakes their fragrant loaf of bread.

Feed each other, tenderly, in the communion of hand and mouth.

Share the meal you've made together.

Play with your creative muse.

Attend to the nature of your relationship with her. Do you dance joyously together? In syncopated rhythm, heart-to-breath-to-body, leaping, twirling, carving gorgeous shapes in the air through which you move?

Does her brilliance overwhelm you? Is she impatient with your slowness, your fumbling, human feet that stumble through the beat? Your need to repeat a step over and over to get its rhythm in your body?

Beguile your muse onto your own stomping grounds. Reveal to her the sweetness of the slow glide, the languid turn. Share the delight of raised dust and pounding feet.

Let her pulse entrain yours to quicksilver. Let the freedom of her limbs, her unfettered heart whirl you through the Milky Way – out to the crackling rim of the universe, into the unknown beyond.

This is the dance. You, squelching her through the glorious muddy pond, the green rustle of meadow. She, steering you in the glittering wake of the stars.

What do you discover, what is revealed, when you bring your worlds together in this way? What can you create together, when you each bring your genius to the dance?

Be home.
Attune to the guardian spirit of your home.
Invite her to grace your life today.

Her arms are filled with gifts for you –
welcome and peace, belonging and nurturance
Divine order, support, love, delight, sovereignty, joy.

Take the gifts she offers, as many as you can hold.
Feel them enliven your home, your heart
with beauty and power.

From the moment you wake until that last flicker of light
before you slip into sleep,
your home holds you in love and blessing.

She is the ground from which you rise each day.
She is the lap of the Sacred, cradling you in tenderness –
shaped by human hands, to grow your human heart.

Whatever your experience of home has been, in the past –
the spirit of home accompanies you now.

Rest in the peace of knowing you are safe –
you are home, you belong.

Move into your world
carrying the power and blessing of home with you.

Be home
for everyone you meet today.

Follow the spirit of adventure, wherever she leads you.

Don't leave a trail of bread-crumbs or pebbles to help you find your way back. Let your curiosity guide you. Let adventure bring you home by pathways you've never explored before.

That thing that you should / ought / gotta do, but aren't doing? Kiss it tenderly and wave goodbye.

Trust the gifts of resistance: Divine timing; right relationship with yourself, your soul, your rambling creativity.

Make friends with patience, with uncertainty.

Today, embrace your meandering, stuttering progress. Trust your soul – it's spinning a dance whose choreography your body knows.

An umbilical cord links your personal power to the deep Sources of all power. Act on the promptings of your soul, and your every action is nurtured by wisdom, discernment, blessing and love.

Today, notice those aspects of your life where you feel like an ant trying to carry an elephant: Small, powerless, overwhelmed, staggering under the weight of responsibility.

Attune now to the pulse of wholeness, within your body and all around you. Its steady flow adds power and presence to whatever you choose to do. Act with its help, and ease, simplicity, miraculous support show up for you. Elephant carries ant.

Just for today, practice acting in partnership with the powers of wholeness.

That thing that lurks in the background of your consciousness – the murky something you catch glimpses of before it disappears into the shadows again? Ask it to meet you, face to face.

As long as it remains back there in the dim corridors of your awareness, it exerts an energetic pull that's out of proportion to its true significance in your life. And, it distorts your energy field in ways that aren't healthy for you or your soul.

Face it directly; see it clearly. Discern the quality of its presence.

What does it show you about itself? What does it need/want/desire?

Is it yours? If it isn't, send it to where it belongs. If it is yours, get to know it. Invite your soul to restore it to its essence, and to its rightful place in your inner ecology. Notice what happens when you do this.

Be the mirror.

Let Grace have her way with you.

Make friends with the question that's knocking on the door of your heart. Embrace the beauty, depth, playfulness and complexity of the world it opens up for you.

Give / offer from a brimming heart.

Receive / take from a generous heart.

Stand barefoot where the tide turns – giving / receiving / giving...

Relinquish elevation. Choose buoyancy.

*

Tune into one decision you've avoided making because you don't know what to do. Feel yourself standing at the crossroads – facing paths that seem to meander off in wildly different directions.

Now, turn to face your soul. Invite it into relationship with the landscape before you – including those pathways that aren't yet visible to you.

Let your soul show you the path that harmonizes most closely with the pattern your soul holds for the perfect unfolding of your life in this situation.

If the path it reveals to you feels daunting – its terrain impossibly steep, fearfully perilous – ask your soul to gather those resources and allies who will help you traverse it with ease.

Then set forth in your chosen direction, one courageous step at a time.

Be a poem.

Plant yourself in the center of the field where sky kneels on the fertile horizon. Put your ear to the ground.

Listen for the wingbeats of new stories, borne on invisible currents.

Your heart a beacon, illuminate a flightpath for them. Guide them to safe landing. Welcome them home.

❖

Celebrate the threads woven by your ancestors into the net that holds your life.

Celebrate the daily web you weave that cradles all of our children in love and mercy, in the tensile strength of our miraculous world.

Nestle into the lap that holds you in safety and tenderness.

Gravity. Grace.

Make a lap for someone else.

Gravity. Grace. Safety. Tenderness.

❖

Take a stand – for truth, justice, beauty, love, wholeness. Stand for that which your heart knows is essential to your well-being, and to the well-being of our world. Stand for the world in which you want to live.

❄

Be the stillness that flows into dance.

Be the hand of freedom that sculpts your art.

Be moonlight on the midnight sea.

Today, as I do every day, I've been recalibrating the cells in the body of Mama Earth. The elements have lost their organically harmonious relationship with each other. Water and earth cower under the ferocity of fire run amok. Air compressed and isolated balloons outward and turns poisonous. Cell walls lose their integrity, their ability to take in and hold nourishment, to filter out toxic intrusion. They burst, bleeding away earth's life-force.

The earth holds the pattern for her own healing and wholeness. We can help, with every choice we make. Our species contributes heavily to the health or dis-ease of our planetary home. Heal your own cells first. Bring the elements in your body into harmony with each other. Fill them with your soul's radiance, with the pattern that your soul holds for their perfect unfolding.

Harmonize with the ecology in which you live. Be an agent of love and Divine Order. See each cell in the body of the earth returning to its natural shape and form. Know each cell as radiant life, fulfilling its divine purpose, in perfect communion with all the other cells that make up the body of the earth.

Do this as an everyday practice. It will transform you, restore right relationship with the earth which is our home. And, it will return our planet to its natural state of grace, power, beauty and harmony.

❋

Write the story of the last day of your life. Live it today.

Take the wildly scenic route. When you spot Serendipity on the side of the road, stop and give her a ride. Let her guide you to your destination.

Dive down that rabbit-hole, head-first. Crawl through twisting tunnels, into the glittering depths of underground caverns. Find your home in the belly of the earth.

Rest here.

Who are you, in this place that pulses with earth's breath, earth's heartbeat?

Remembrance of moonlight in a dark so complete you're back in mama's womb, being breathed, arteries flushing red with each syncopated heartbeat.

Invite curiosity to lead the way. Let the blessed rain of understanding put out the fires of judgment and condemnation.

*

Release all your agendas – set them free.

Improvise.

Let the wind carry you. Just for this moment. And maybe the next.

Invite the burning questions, the knotted, difficult, painful questions, into your belly, into your heart. Give them room to stretch out to their full height and depth; room to breathe, to sing, to be.

Who are you, in relationship to these questions? What and how do you feel, in their presence? How do these questions feel, as visitors in your world? Do they feel safe enough to express their beauty, their power, their complexity?

What can you and these questions reveal to each other – about who you both are, about your world?

Open wide. Listen. Share yourselves. Explore. Discover something new.

When you feel the intimate breath of your questions on your cheek, when you know them the way your heart knows the blood that pulses in and through it, then act on their behalf. Act on your shared knowing.

❖

Turn down the volume. Shhhhhhh...

In the clear silence, listen for the pulse of your soul. Listen for the heartbeat of Divine Order, shaping a new wholeness.

Listen, before you act.

Your soul's call summons all the powers of wholeness – the Soul of Humanity, the Soul of the World – to our collective task of healing, peacemaking, and renewal.

Listen for what's being asked of you. Listen – then act as only you can. Do the thing that's yours to do.

Wrap yourself in the consciousness of a cloud, belly brimming with rain, sun dappling through you, blue sky at your back, around you, above you, within you, beyond your arms' reach.

Run, run with the wind. Empty your heart on city streets, muddy fields. Pour your treasure into the waiting arms of trees, the silver capillaries of rivers.

Give all you are, all you hold. Then dissolve, dissolve. Become invisible.

❋

Whatever you've chosen to create or participate in, give it all you've got. Love it wholeheartedly. Cherish its unfolding life. Then, step back and let it find its own way home.

❖

Notice where the flow of power and presence is impeded in your life.

Meet this impediment without judgment, with openness and curiosity. Get to know it. Seek to understand its nature, its beliefs about the world, how it functions, what purpose it serves in the ecology of your life.

Invite your soul into relationship with this log-jam in the river of your power and presence. Nothing to do. Just hold a space of possibility and willingness, as your soul does its work of reconfiguring the flow of your life.

Notice what happens to the impediment, to the flow. Notice how you feel as the log-jam clears, as flow is restored.

When you feel complete, for now, notice where your power and presence want to flow.

What action will you take, spontaneously, powerfully, to be the current of the world? How will you contribute to shaping the world in which you want to live?

Trace the arc of freedom you've reclaimed through your experiences of being bound.

How did your enslavement – to economic or political structures, to thought-forms and beliefs, to ideologies and the elites who perpetuate them, to anything or anyone that intervenes between you and your soul – shape your path to freedom?

What can you share, from your experience, with a world struggling to be free? How will you use your freedom to support the lives of all who would be free?

Which great river are you waiting to cross? No matter how fragile your boat, become part of the ecology of the river and it will carry you to the far shore. One paddle-stroke at a time.

＊

Let events school you. Change your mind. Choose the direction that calls to your heart today.

Close the doors that no longer lead to your soul's desires.

Remember when you were a child, and a tree was a wondrous being of dappled light and swaying shadows on sticky summer afternoons?

Remember the feel of barkskin and sap stinging the palms of your hands, rubbing against the soles of your feet. The sharp green scent of leaves rustling all around you as you climbed the branching ladder of the tree's many arms.

Remember how you loved that tree, how you loved who you were, curled in the nest of its canopy.

Remember how you loved the world beneath you, a magic carpet undulant with promise, the wind swinging you high in your hammock of green and gold.

That tree was home and beauty, outlook and adventure, a sailing ship on a sea of sky. It was Tree. Its whispers lingered in your dreams, those fragrant nights of childhood summer.

When did tree's glory dim and recede? It remains true to itself – taller, fuller, stouter, but still tree. What's changed, in your relationship with it?

When did you slip into the story in which tree is Resource, to be managed, cultivated, exploited for its timber or its bark? When did it become a precursor to paper, to firewood, to the frame of your house, the turned legs of your dining room table? Or one more thing you are responsible for – leaves to be raked in the fall, branches to be pruned in early spring.

When did you stop loving Tree for its tree-ness? When did you stop loving yourself for your self-ness? Can you trace the pathways by which this happened?

When did you slip into the story in which you – your beauty, your joy, your eager heart, your creative blaze – became a repository for desires not your own; a screen for the projections of society and culture.

When did you allow a half-blind world to describe you to yourself?

What strange, reverse alchemy transformed you from beloved to resource – to be exploited, tamed, cultivated, packaged? Even – especially – by you?

Stop. Turn around. Retrace your steps. Climb back into the tree of your being, feeling your own rough bark, your sticky sap, in the palms of your hands, on the soles of your feet.

Discover the secrets of your hidden chambers, your musk and music, your seasons of longing, your surging desires, your shivering joys.

Who are you, O creature of love and music, of branching arms and sunburnt hair? This is your journey. Back to yourself. Back to loving heartwood and sap, bark and leaf, ear-shell, blood-tide, breath-wind, galvanized skin on muscular flesh. You.

Let the touch of the world on your skin be the golden honey of love. Let sunlight stream love through your face, your chest, your throat, your knees, your feet. Let wind caress your hair with exquisite, playful tenderness.

You are the beloved of the world. Receive love with radiant hands.

❖

Surrender your plans, your hopes and fears, your desires and dreams, your heartaches and longings – for yourself, for your loves, for your world. Lay them all at the feet of the Beloved. Surrender them to the flow that carries you into the heart of your belonging.

Surrender your will to the pattern that the Great Architect has inscribed for you on the map of creation.

Let your soul be your guide, your heart's faithful companion.

❋

Play with your ability to flex and stretch – your body, your mind, your heart, your point of view.

Play with edges and boundaries. Push them out further; move them in closer. Soften them; firm them up. Infuse them with light, with shade, with fierce love, with playful truth.

Pay attention to your discoveries. Who are you, when you bushwhack your way into unknown terrain? What do you discover about your world, and your place in it? How much fun can you have, playing flex-and-stretch?

Be impeccable with your word. Choose your commitments wisely, then do what you say you're going to do, even if you don't feel like it, even if it's hard.

There are no inconsequential choices. Each promise fulfilled grows your capacity to hold and express your soul's formidable power. Each commitment honoured strengthens your ability to serve wholeness, to be an effective agent of love, kindness, generativity and truth.

Gather your power. Place it in service to your soul's joy. Your word is the Sacred, sounding the world into being.

❋

Immerse the hard, the painful, the stubbornly stuck in the lofting alchemy of humour. Spin the story upside down, inside out – shake rattle and roll the bones of truth. Let the wisdom of absurdity levitate you.

❖

Attune to the abundant beauty, love, power and miracles that are dancing on your doorstep. Welcome them in – into your home, into your heart, your life, your business.

Be the miracle that embraces the abundance of the universe intimately, wholeheartedly, with tender devotion.

Be the miracle of joyous abundance for everyone you meet today.

❋

Turn up your radiance. Let it illuminate the path before you as you take the next steps to light up your world.

Offer the wisdom you've distilled from your own suffering as nectar and balm to heal the world's wounds.

All of your experiences have led you to this place – you have become the gift your world needs in order to become whole. You have risen, like good bread, from being kneaded, hard, by life's knuckles. You have breathed through broken ribs and burning lungs to become soul food, to become a source of pure nourishment.

You know, from your own rising, how to alchemize what ails our world – how to transform divisiveness, fear, despair, violence, slavery, suffering into the nectar of love.

You are the bread of freedom. Go, feed your world today.

Make a bonfire of your identities.

Write them on slips of paper, all these ideas you hold about yourself, all these beliefs you've chosen or inherited, accepted, clung to or fought against. I am _____, and _____, and _____.

Bring them to the clear blue flame of your soul's boundless truth. Place them in its fire – watch them burn. Watch them curl into smoke, leaving no residue behind.

Say goodbye. Grieve the loss of who you've been, the loss of your ideas about yourself, about your place in the world.

Breathe the sweet breath of freedom. It may feel cold, at first, too rarefied for lungs accustomed to the tar of deprivation. Breathe anyway. Breathe until you know yourself as freedom, as truth, as the hand of justice, the heart of the universe.

You are the Sacred incarnate. Know the creative power of who you are, with each in-breath. Give yourself to your world with each out-breath.

Know this in the whoosh of your blood, in the temple of your bones. Know it in your salty sweat, in the honey of your cells. You are the Mystery made flesh. There is no other like you, on this earth – no other inhabits your form, lives in your shape.

You are the essence of the Beloved, in the shape of you. The infinite in your particular heartbeat. Take That into your day.

Loosen the fists of self-righteousness; lay down the dagger of judgement.

Discernment strokes truth's soft cheeks with loving hands, with precise, gentle fingertips.

Your heart reveals what's real – the Beloved's face in everyone, in everything you encounter today.

The rest is just noise, just the sound of simooms sighing through canyons of forgetting.

Turn down the volume. Meet the wonder that you are, face-to-face.

❈

Notice where you're mistaking the holes in the net for the sky. Untangle yourself from the struggle by simply stepping away. Let the strength of your wings loft you as high as you wish to fly.

As you cleanse your inner being of all that muddies the clear currents of your soul, the things that once supported and served you may now become boulders in the stream of your incarnation.

Thank these helpers for their loving kindness, for the precious gifts they offered to your becoming. Bless them – and release them.

Who you are today is not who you were yesterday. Feel the movements of your soul sculpting new riverbanks to hold the flow of your life now.

Where and how does this gathering power want to express itself? How will you activate it to serve and bless the becoming of your world today?

※

Make a living cathedral of green groves and overarching trees inside yourself. Let joy's songs of praise & celebration reverberate through every cell of your body.

Who are you, when your primary vibration is joy? How do you meet and marry your world, with joy as your heart's companion?

Joy is the essence of your DNA. It's a quality of soul, ever-present in you, offering itself at every turn. Embrace it as you would your next breath, your beloved, your own faithful, beating heart.

Be the hum and hymn of joy in your world today.

Tune into the crests and troughs of the waves that you're riding right now – the slip-sliding micro-movements of your life.

Feel the nature of each phase of the wave – the bright billowing surge, its sunlit crown foaming against the force of gravity; the swift plunge into a coldly swirling unknown.

Experience fully the vibrational nature of each of these states of being. Savour the precise differences that make each of them unique.

Explore the relationship between them. Ride the movement of the wave; feel how it functions – that moment when ascent becomes descent, when crest begins the slide back to trough, when apogee swells towards rise.

Hold each of these phases of movement in the cupped palms of your hands – rise in one, fall in the other. They are both form and function. Feel their heft and texture, the hot and cold of them, the density and loft of their restless, expressive life.

Move your hands in the dance of their co-mingling. Let the movement travel from your hands through your arms, from your arms through your body. Feel, in your whole body, this movement of rise and fall, swell and slide, this undulant life.

What do you know now, that you didn't know before you entered this dance? What do you know about the movements of your cells, of your blood, your nerves, your breath? How do you experience the surge and ebb of your life now?

What do you know about the movements of your world – the ones that elate or frustrate you; the ones that scoop you through the waves of hope and despair?

What will you do with this knowledge? How does it change your relationship to power, to action? How will you embody and direct the power of this movement today?

※

Play with pairs of opposites. Hold joy in one hand, sorrow in the other. Power in your left hand, powerlessness in your right. Compassion/ Judgement. Truth/Dissembling.

Bring them together, these two faces of the same essential soul quality. Bring your hands together in prayer mudra, feel these opposites commingling in your heart, which knows how to hold both-and in a welcoming embrace.

Other pairings? Tune into the ones that are most vividly present in your life right now. As you play with them, explore the ease with which you can shift energetic states, from one to the other and back again. Then, immerse yourself in the essential harmony from which they emerge.

Who are you, and what do you bring to your world when you practice this alchemy as naturally as breathing in and breathing out?

Simplicity.

Complex systems – like our miraculous bodies, our lives, our businesses, our world – function beautifully through simplicity. There's grace and power in simplicity. It harmonizes opposing forces by focusing on the unifying essence of their being.

Today, choose simplicity. Moment-to-moment, let every encounter with your world – inner, outer – be simple, direct, filled with ease.

What changes – in you, in the choices you make, in your relationship with your world – when you meet each moment from the heart of simplicity?

As you move through your day, meet yourself and the world around you from this one radiant truth: You are a miracle. Everyone and everything else is, too.

Attune to the field of miracles in your own body – in each breath; in the whoosh of blood through your arteries and veins; in your beating heart; the delicate tracery of your nerves; the rise and fall of your skin; your infinite mind, your tender soul.

See with miraculous eyes. Hear with miraculous ears. Speak the miracle of words, listen with the soft ears of wordlessness.

What happens when you – in all your miraculous being – embrace the miraculous world, one fluid moment at a time? What happens when you eat a golden pear, breathe the green air under a tree, stroke your beloved's cheek, sing your world to sleep, give and receive and give and receive in the field of miracles?

What miracles will you participate in creating today? For yourself? For someone you love? For your dreaming, aching world?

Touch the web of creation with your fully charged fingertip. Set something in motion that reverberates from where you stand to the places and people who have forgotten the truth you embody today. Discover what happens next...

You are one of the original architects of our planet, Earth. You hold the vision and pattern for the perfect unfolding of this blue-green beauty, and for its relationship with all forms of life in its care, but you, yourself, have never incarnated.

What do you know, that will heal, transform, restore and bless our Earth today? What do you know that will help it flow into the vision and pattern you hold for its unfolding?

Who are your incarnate allies – human, animal, vegetable, mineral – who have already established pathways through which your vision is taking shape and form? What kinds of partnership and support do they need from you, to act in the physical world?

Who are your subtle-energy allies, and how do you work with them to create the synergy necessary for restoring the earth to wholeness?

What commitments will you make, as a result of what you know? What action or actions will you take today, to bring this vision down to earth?

✳

Release it all, with love. Let everything flow through you like a clear spring running down a mountainside.

Let Love irrigate your life to a fine fertility.

Lighten up.

What feels like too-much-of-a-muchness right now? Too heavy, too ornate, out-of-sync with who you are today?

You wouldn't put a Gerhard Richter painting in a baroque frame. Nor load a skiff with a cargo of gold.

Notice those elements in your life that are excessive, that no longer belong with you, that throw the ecology of your life off-keel. The things that once were at the center of your world, but now feel strangely askew.

Relationships that have grown stale or run their course. Vision that once was a beckoning horizon and now is opaque, shuttered. Ways of living and working that were ballast, and now are simply dead weight.

What needs to be refreshed, renewed? What relinquished entirely?

Take the action that restores buoyancy, loft, joy. Take the action that feathers your wings.

Dive in. Feel your muscles tremble and contract. Feel your sip-shallow breath flutter high in your chest as you hover over the abyss, your bare toes gripping the cliff-edge of your next creative adventure.

Wrap your arms around yourself, in love, in tenderness. Breathe, deep into your belly – let your lungs remind you of the improbable miracle of your life. Remember, you are safe – you have done brave and difficult things. You know how to do this too.

You are not alone. Look around you. Feel the powerful love that holds you, from all the beloveds who know you, who believe in you, who have your back.

Call on the powers of wholeness, summon the spirit of courage. Feel the great wind of your soul rocket you to your chosen destiny.

O flying spark of Divine radiance, dive in! Dive in.

Let the world and your engagement with it flow outside the silken cocoon of your sleep. Enter dreamtime with a clear intention – whatever is closest to your heart tonight.

To rest deeply and renew each cell in your body to its most vibrant potential.

To explore the mysteries of the universe with no agenda other than the joy of discovery.

To mine the gold of wisdom in response to a question that's been whispering in your ear all day.

To learn about your art, or meet with your Muse for a very specific purpose.

To grow new, tender shoots in your soul's garden.

To have tea and cake with your tribe of elders and Devas in the subtle energy realms.

To play with your beloved in the field of miracles.

Whatever your intention, declare it, sing it out loud, whisper it to the stars. Then, release it into the creative flow of the universe, and sleep. Sleep, knowing you've done your part.

Let wholeness meet you at the threshold of the blessed dark.

❊

You are a living cell in the body of the world. You are the hands and feet of the Sacred on this earth.

How does this knowledge shape your relationship with everything and everyone you encounter today? How does it inform your choices and actions, as you move through your day?

Fold this truth into your intentions for today. Then, as night falls and sleep beckons, feel the love you've become at the end of the day. Feel the transformations that happened within you, and in your world, as a result of living this truth.

Close your eyes and turn all the way around, slow-w-ly. Sense or feel the open door, the one that offers you ease, that welcomes you to a new homecoming.

Walk up to this doorway, still with your eyes closed. Feel the grain of the threshold under your feet, the doorjamb beneath the palm of your hand. Feel the life pulsing on the other side, offering itself to you.

When you're ready, step through. Breathe this new air. Feel who you are, in this unknown, deeply familiar place. Feel how you stand, how your feet hold and are held by the ground here.

Feel yourself welcomed, embraced, in all of your beauty and timidity, your power and grace. Feel all that this place holds for you and with you.

Ask those questions that glow steadily in your heart. Here are the ones that arise to my lips in this liminal space.

Why am I here?

How truly do I love?

What is yearning to be born?

How do I serve now?

How do I love my world now?

Stay here for as long as you wish. When you feel complete, for now, ask this place for a talisman, a reminder that the door is open for you, that welcome and belonging await you there, as they do here.

Turn around, and step back into the present moment, bringing the gifts of this place with you. Place your talisman on your altar, or in the altar of your heart. Kiss it, bless it, be blessed by it.

Write a note, a promise to yourself, to your soul, to your world: This is what I will do to live where I'm being called, to live where I belong.

Then, gather your allies and resources. Make a plan. Put it into motion. Begin today.

❊

Your hands are embodied grace, living expressions of nurturance and blessing.

Anytime you touch something today – your child's face, your computer key-board, your chair or desk, the lamp beside your bed, the food you put into your mouth – touch it with the full power of the love that you are. Let the tenderness in your heart overflow into your hands. Feel your hands alive with love. Let every touch be a joyous communion of love, delight, beauty and blessing.

At the end of the day, notice what's changed in you. What's different about your world after a day of conscious, loving touch?

It's Fall, here in my neck of the woods – the season when Light turns from summer-shaded eyes and sun-blessed skin to begin her steep descent through the corridor of bones, into the cold, slow marrow of winter. Season of drifting leaves, of trees returning their green-gold life to their ancient roots.

Today, play with falling. Play with it on the floor of your dance studio, your yoga mat, your soft, soft bed. Better yet, rake up a great pile of leaves, and fall into them.

As you fall, feel the rush and whoosh and gasp of letting gravity have her way with you. Savour the tickle of leaves in your nose, their cushiony crunch, their peaty breath enfolding you. With your back smooshed into piles of leaves, breathe in; breathe out. Feel your heart slowing to a steady drumbeat. Feel the cradle of grace that is your breath, rocking you.

With each breath in, feel the lungs of the world breathing for you. With each breath out, feel the earth breathing with you. Feel yourself being breathed in utter safety – a child cradled in falling leaves, cradled in the lap of the world.

Safely held, you are free to play. You can climb. You can fly. You can fall. You can lift. You can drop, tumble, roll, let go. Feel your heart race as you climb, as you launch yourself from that highest branch. Fly! Wheeee! Fall! Whooosh!

Fall into safety. Fall into lift and loft and tumble, into scratch and soft and thump and rustle. Fall into freedom.

Let the feeling of falling shake your limbs, limber your heart. Let it swing you by the hand through the enchantment of the day. Know this, in your bones – you're free to fall, and rise, and fall again, climb, leap, fly again.

Let your mind mimic your body's freedom. Loosen your grip on the things that vex you. Let them fall, too. Let them fall.

Fall for the joy of it! Fall for the joy!

❄

That big, complex vision you're in the midst of making real? Tune into the simplicity at its heart.

The essence of any creation is love. Tune into the love that first called you to Yes. Before your creation became a project, before it ever took shape and form, it was a Beloved.

Let love restore the magic that guides your vision to its birth. Let love welcome every vista, cave and tunnel along the way. Let love quarry and lay each stone with supreme artistry and devotion, to build the temple of your desire. Then, invite the people in.

Consider the thing that's been tugging at your heart lately. Something that hasn't quite come into focus. A dream. A wish. A desire. A sense that makes no sense, yet feels as intimate as the inside of your belly.

Its outlines are blurry, its power undeniable.

Play with it from different vantage points. Draw it in close – so close, you can taste its breath, feel the zing of it raise the tiny hairs on your arms. So close you can't tell whose heartbeat thuds in your chest, whose pulse whooshes in your veins.

Now pull back – take it in whole, from across the room. Its slouchy stance, that jut of jaw and hip. Those waves of delight that roll across the floor like a tsunami headed straight for your heart.

Pull back further: To the rooftop, treetop, mountaintop. Pull all the way back to fill the sky. Feel the pull between you, elastic as taffy, stretching, stretching. Never breaking. Stay there, in that current of connection...

Until you're pulled back in again, facing each other, close but not so close that you can't see yourself. Or it. This thing that's been tugging at your heart. Calling your name. Calling you to know it, to love it, to wrap it around you. To bring it to life so you can play, and play some more. Together.

Where do you need to stand, today, to bring it into being? Do you want it in your life? If the answer is Yes, what will you do to make a home for it, today?

Remove the hook of approval from the inside of your mouth. Gently, gently, so the barb doesn't rip your tender flesh.

Remove the hook of disapproval from the hollow of your throat. Gently, patiently, with infinite care. Soften the muscles of your throat until that hook slips out without doing further damage.

Return them, approval and disapproval, hook, line and sinker, to the great void that dissolves all forms.

Irrigate your mouth, your throat, with the lavage of kindness. As the wounds in your body close, seal them with kisses, bandage them in love.

Who are you, when you're no longer hooked on approval, caught on the fishing line of disapproval? How tall do you stand? How wide is your heart? How deep is your breath?

Move through your day filling your lungs with the sweet air of freedom. Follow the call of your true desires, moment to moment, and discover where they lead you.

Open pathways through which that which is calling you can stream into your world. Stand in the field of your desire. Feel its resonance and power in your breath, the flow of rich blood in your arteries and veins, in the hum of your bones, in the joyous song that rises from every cell in your body.

Feel the earth cradling you in her lap, the cosmos wheeling its galaxies in your belly.

Face each of the ten directions in turn. Call on the Devas of each direction to create a sphere of power and presence with you. Invite the Devas of Birth, Flow, Form and Provision into this sphere. Ask them to open pathways of light through which all that belongs with you can dance into your world.

Add veils at the portals to these pathways, so they are only visible to love and the sources of love.

Open your arms. Welcome your desires home.

Wash away the imprints on your skin, on your heart, of other people's desires, expectations, fears, hopes, demands and projections.

You may never know whence they came, or to whom they belong. Yet they exert a pressure on your energy field to conform to the shape of their deliriums. They form a barrier between you and your soul.

You may experience them as lethargy, confusion, fuzziness, lack of direction, bewilderment. Not knowing what you want or being unable to reach your joy, your enthusiasm. Or feelings of hopelessness, anhedonia.

Notice the nature of these imprints and their effects on you, and wash them away as simply as you wash away the grime of the day. No need to create stories about them, or to judge, blame, resist or cling to them. Feel the steam of the great cosmic shower dissolve them – whoooshh! Gone!

Feel the pores of your skin open to inhale your soul's tender joy. Feel the bell of truth ring and ring in your heart. Welcome home, welcome home.

Saturate yourself with sensual pleasure.

Sun on your skin, or rain, or wind. A book, a poem that opens your wings. Fragrant tea by firelight. Laughter.

Paint, bare hands glopped in crimson and gold. Sing in the shower. Sing from your jelly belly.

Light quivering through autumn leaves. Colour, radiance. Texture. Fingertips tracing feathers across the jut of your shoulders. Music. Sweet humming silence. Love in every form. Pleasure.

Explore. Discover what pleases you. Give yourself to that. Romance your world. Come home to your senses.

❋

Notice where you're leaning outside of yourself to reach for your desires. Tremulous, held-breath, tip-toe, afraid you'll fall over because you're reaching beyond your centre of gravity.

Bring yourself back – back to your soul, your breath, your body, your heart. Back to your centre of power and presence.

Your desires are not out there in the magical beyond. You cannot grasp them or bind them to you by pursuing them as they flee towards some illusory horizon.

The power to fulfill your desire doesn't lie outside of you. It's not held in the palm of someone else's hands, to be bestowed upon you or withheld. It doesn't depend on caprice or will. Your desire cannot be fulfilled by appeasing the gods of bestowal.

Your true desires are expressions of your soul. They are road maps to the paths of your unfolding incarnation. Every true desire is your soul showing you those aspects of itself it wants to bring into being.

Meet your desire as you meet your soul, because that is what it is. Embrace it with love, joy and tenderness, with curiosity and delight.

Let each desire show you the You that it holds in the cradle of its heart. Let your soul open the pathways through which your desire blooms and flowers within you, delivering the fragrance of its own fulfillment.

Do you really believe that your infinite soul – which has created and dissolved a million different forms and incarnations – lacks the power to unfold the miracles it conjures for you?

Be in right relationship with the weather. If it's blustery and raining today, be the sun. If it's sunny today, be the wind, or a cloud, or a rainbow, or whatever you please. If the weather's changing from hour to hour, play with movement, mutability – or be the ballast that steadies a fluctuating world.

❋

Relinquish grievance for grief. Cynicism for sorrow. Blame for bewilderment. Righteousness for ravishment.

What happens when you descend from the mountaintop to enter the cave of matter?

Serenade your soul. Sing like a river, your body a leaping, yielding, shimmering current of liquid passion. Sing with your whole rapturous, over-the-moon-in-love heart. Invite your soul to dance with you. Cheek to cheek, belly to belly. To your song.

*

Get clear on what's true for you. Then, act on it with strength and courage.

When you choose your soul's path, Grace accompanies you. She smooths the way, enriches and makes fertile the soil of your life. Your reward is an authentic life, a peaceful, spacious, joyous heart.

You are a gift. Receiving is a soul art. How you're received isn't up to you, though it may leave you feeling more or less gifted. Feel your feelings. Then, use your discernment to choose where, when and for whom you show up.

Let nothing diminish the truth of your inner knowing – you are a gift.

Notice where in your life you habitually stoop to walk beneath low-hanging branches.

Is there some other way you can act? Walk around them? Leap over them? Choose an entirely different route? Greet them with friendly appreciation and lift them out of your way as you pass by?

What transformation takes place in you, when you change the habit of stooping?

Listen! The stars in the belly of the earth are singing your name.
Entrust your heart to the singers who welcome you home.

＊

Love what is.

Love the painful, prickly, knotted, difficult, pig-headed, intractable. Love what grates on your nerves, love the sensation of grating, love the fine-tuned fretwork of your nerves.

Love the fluid, light, strong, glorious, playful, brilliant. Love what enchants and delights you. Love what makes your heart as soft as dawn, as wide as the sky. Love fierce and tender, peaceful and wrathful. Love muscular, flexible, powerful. Love birth and death in all creation.

Nothing changes without love. The true nature of all things is love – everything opens into the fullness of its being in the light of love. If you want a kinder, more just world, or a kinder world inside your own heart and belly, love what is, today.

It's the day after your death. Feel into the You who inhabits this liminal space.

Who are you now? What do you experience? Explore yourself and your surroundings lightly, playfully. Be curious.

Where are you? What's your relationship with your once-upon-a-time body? With the life you've just left behind?

What's your relationship with the people and places that were seminal to your incarnation? Who and what and how do you love, in your present state of being? What's your relationship with the earth, the sun, the moon, the stars? Where do they reside, in your newly liberated consciousness?

Who accompanies you, in this stage of your journey? Where and with whom do you belong?

What do you know now, that you didn't know back then, when you were living in the midst of your incarnate story?

Play with this exploration for as long as you wish. When you've had enough, for now, return to your body, to your breath, to your present. Pat yourself all over. Dance, or walk or run – whatever calls to you.

Bring back with you the qualities of being that you discovered on your travels into your future. Let the flavour of that experience perfume your choices and the flow of your energy today.

You've carried a sack of spiny mollusks on your back for most of your life – for many lifetimes. Their smelly heft, their unpredictably shifting, jostling weight, the sudden jabs they deliver through the sack's rough weave, keep you always on edge, even when the path beneath your feet is smooth and welcoming.

Today, put this sack down by the side of the road.

Feel your shoulders – braced, for so long, against their jagged burden – drop, twitch a little, drop some more. Feel the strain in your back, your neck, your head, ease, bit by cautious bit, as you walk away into the rest of your life.

Feel your breath grow deeper, fuller. Feel your arms relax, unclench their grip. Feel your fingers lengthen, one by one, taking back their natural shape and form. Feel the arches of your feet release into a lower register. Feel your toes lengthen to an organic relationship with the ground.

Who are you, unburdened now, set free by choice and action? How do you experience the shifts in your organs, your bones, your muscles and tendons, the way your body stands and moves and carves the air around you?

Explore the freedom that lives on the other side of this divestment. Dance, skip, lunge, leap, sing, cry, laugh, twirl. Do whatever you feel moved to do. Express yourself – share who you are with your world.

❖

Take your most cherished assumptions out to play. Spend the afternoon with them. Build sandcastles, or bike together on your favourite mountain trail. Make art, or make luscious edible delights to feast on at teatime.

Be curious. Get to know them, these assumptions that have snuggled in the back of your closet or under your bed all these years. Do you like hanging out with them? Are they fun to be with? Are they spontaneous as two-year-olds, game for adventure, greedy for new experiences? Do they love dreaming and doing and exploring with you? Do they get sweaty in the sun? Muddy and happy or scowly and furious when it rains?

Are they as real as your heartbeat, as twitchy as the tip of your nose? Can you kiss their cheeks? If you ask, will they give you a piggyback ride, or laugh with you until your stomachs hurt? Do they come home with you tonight, flushed, dishevelled, sunburned, as sturdy as a herd of horses? Or do they melt, disappear like phantoms, like mist?

What do you know about your assumptions, after a whole day of hanging out together?

*

That one wiggly, barely-hanging-by-a-thread tooth that you keep probing with your tongue even though it hurts and bleeds and tastes of copper and panic each time you touch it... That.

Feel the wobbliness and zing of it. Feel the ways in which it sizzle-brands pathways of pain, adrenalized avoidance, irresistible attraction throughout your body. That shaky, oh-my-god-this-hurts-I-can't-believe-I'm-doing-this-again feeling that leaves you breathless, a little sick, ashamed, agonized – again.

Take a breath. Let it go. Another breath. In. Out. In. Out. In...Out...

Let the metronome of your breath restore you to your senses.

Explore the relationship between the Thing That Hurts, the You That Hurts, and the You that keeps pressing on the thing that keeps hurting.

You're exploring what is, rather than what has been – probing biology, not history. Your history shapes your biology, but what you choose to practice today, and every day from here on, becomes your history, becomes your biology.

Drop your gaze down into the cavity of your body. In and under and between the zing of pain, the swirls of panic, where do you hold the You that is steady, calm, patient, sure-footed? Tune into the You that is loving, courageous, open-hearted, reliably kind.

Feel the texture and flavour, the warmth or coolness, the heft and buoyancy of your powerful self. Feel it in the steadiness of your heartbeat, in the calm center of your belly, in the strength of your thighs – wherever your joy, your wisdom, your generosity and power live, within you.

This feeling is energy, and energy is mostly empty space. Bring your awareness into the empty spaces inside the feeling of steady strength, reliable kindness, in your body. Expand your soul's presence throughout these spaces, filling them with your radiance, with your soul's light.

Notice what happens when you do this. Notice the quality of your breath, the pattern of your thoughts, the sensations in your body, the feelings that arise and dissolve in your belly, in your heart.

Now, from this place of fullness and presence, invite the Thing That Hurts to reveal its heart to you. Ask it to show you where it lives, in your body. Notice its texture, weight, and temperature. Notice the feel of it in your body. Ask it to show you who and what it is, what it hopes for and dreams of, what it needs and desires from you.

Knowing that it is energy, and energy is mostly empty space, expand your soul's presence into the empty spaces inside The Thing That Hurts. Meet it inside itself, with your soul's fullness and presence. You're not trying to cut it off, get rid of it, or change it in any way – you're simply meeting it with all the love and wholeness that is your soul's essence.

Feel what happens, when you do this.

What do you know now, that you didn't know when you entered into this exploration? Feel the texture of your heart. Can you soften it, widen it, let it be as receptive and generous as it really is, even in the face of The Thing That Hurts, The You That Hurts, and The You That Keeps Going Back For More?

If you can soften and allow your heart to be receptive, let it be so. If you can't, and your heart feels rigid, let it be so. Give yourself space and kindness to be where you are right now. Let your willingness lead the way instead.

Be willing to embrace yourself, your feelings, the situation, and the other people involved, with a powerfully loving, spacious, generous heart. What creative responses emerge, from this place within you? How will you use your power to bring a clearer, stronger energy of love and truth into this situation?

❈

Feel the zap and zing of urgency electrifying your body. Feel how it shallows your breath, pushes your pulse, freezes your heart, sears your throat. Feel its insinuation carve a canyon between you and your soul.

Command it to flow out of your body – to show you its true shape and form. What does it look and feel like, this twirling dervish of urgency? Invite it to settle in the palms of your hands. Feel its acid breath, its jumping, jiving, jostling self prancing in the cup of your hands.

Now, fill the bellows of your lungs with clear, sweet air. And blow. Blow that goblin of urgency out to the horizon, and beyond. Blow it out to the edge of the farthest galaxy, and beyond. See it become a speck, a dot, a nothing, as it disappears from view. Erased by the rim of the universe.

Return to the cadence and architecture of your own body. Your breath flowing in and out of your lungs. Your pulse. Your heartbeat. The soft insides of your mouth, the bend of your wrists, the tensile power in the arches of your feet. Rest and flow and dance with the rhythms of your aboriginal body.

Where is your soul in relationship to you now? What will you create, from the depths of your bones?

Explore your relationship with provision. Notice and name all the ways in which you are provided for.

The air you breathe, that powers your lungs and your life, the sun warming your skin, the earth beneath your feet, the magnetic pull of gravity – each of these provides you with elements essential for your life and well-being. Freely given, requiring only your presence, receptivity, and willingness to support the ecology within which provision naturally arises and flows.

Now, notice other currents of provision that circulate in and around you. Your heart and belly are your most receptive organs. How much of the provision that's always available are you willing to receive? How effectively do you digest and integrate the provision that flows into your life?

What aspects of provision do you barricade yourself against, or turn your back upon? What are you afraid will happen if you receive them fully, freely, gratefully? Soften your heart, breathe into your belly. Let your body's wisdom open to receive the sustenance you need.

Where, in your heart and belly, does your longing for provision override your ability to see and receive it? Again – your body knows what kind and quality of provision it needs. It knows how to receive it, digest it, transmute it and offer it, in turn. Let your body take the lead here.

In what ways are you a source of provision for others? Does what you provide for your world overflow from your abundance, or does it feel forced or pinched, or leave you feeling resentful or depleted?

What does right relationship with provision look and feel like for you, now that you've explored it and re-calibrated it in this way?

✳

Notice the inner places where you're holding your breath, walking on eggshells around the living room of your self.

Notice the contraction of your muscles, the hump of your shoulders, the pitch of your pelvis, the way you sip air instead of taking it in freely and fully as a gift of divine grace.

Notice the quality of your being when you scrunch down to be less than the radiant, miraculous, multidimensional human that you are.

How do you feel?

Now, ask yourself this question: Who profits from my diminution? Who – in my life, in my circle of family and friends, in my work, my ancestry, in the historical, political, cultural, social, economic life of my world – profits, when I act from this diminished self? When I become less than all that I am?

Ask yourself a further question: In what ways do I benefit, from this stance? Are the costs of truncating myself in these ways worth the benefits?

Be truthful, with your responses. Take your time. There's no shame or blame involved here, just playful curiosity and willingness to know your truth.

Now, choose. Choose to stand up tall. Choose to open your chest, widen your shoulders, let the weight of your torso rest in the bowl of your pelvis. Choose to entrust the upright wand of your body to the miraculous stability of the soles of your feet.

Declare your sovereignty. Banish the profiteers from your kingdom. Bring those of your inner selves who have grown accustomed to a hunched-over life, back into your heart, back into the safety of your love and belonging, back into a clear-eyed orientation to your world.

Choose your power. Choose the power of your full presence. Choose to be the light of your world.

Be radiant. Then, radiate.

❖

Trust gravity enough to tread lightly, lightly through the landscape of your life. Trust your soul and the soul of the world enough to yield your gifts courageously, wholeheartedly, to the task at hand.

There are invisible forces in play that lend their power to every action we take, individually and collectively, to untangle discord and weave patterns of harmony, peace and sacred order.

Listen for what's being asked of you. Then, step in with willing heart and radiant hands to share in the Great Weaving of the world.

Calibration calls for infinite patience. And faith. Faith is abiding – every breath is both an act and a proof of faith. Patience, on the other hand... she's elusive. Patience wants wooing.

Some days, I have more faith than patience.

Patience is twin sister to faith. Both know that the god of love arrives when he will, and cannot be summoned – only welcomed, embraced with glad tears and deep delight.

Together, patience and faith make a home for love. They listen for his footfall, watch for his warm breath in the clear, cold air, confident that when the lamps are lighted and the fire burning in the hearth, good bread and soup laid on the table, love will follow his own winged footsteps home.

❋

Healing is tidal and undulant – rise and fall, ebb and flow, surge and recede are inherent in its nature, and essential to its functioning.

It's a skill and art to be in right relationship with healing. The more closely you attune to its rhythms and harmonize with them, the more fluid the healing process will be.

If you hang onto one aspect of it too long, while it has already moved into another, you create obstruction and suffering.

Pay attention to the overall pattern of healing, even as you surf the wave that surges or recedes within you, and you'll know that the ocean of grace that carries you is the true matrix of healing.

Divine Order is always present, even when it seems invisible. It's always available to us, as a template and guide. We can choose to attune to it, to let it strengthen and inform our becoming. In times of profound uncertainty, it is the clearer, stronger frequency that leads us home.

The more chaotic the world around us becomes, the greater the need for each of us to embody Divine Order, in our own lives, in the body politic, and in our world.

Try it. Discover for yourself what happens when you attune to the frequency of Divine Order and let it harmonize your cellular structure, your bones, muscles, nerves and arteries, your heart, your thoughts, feelings, choices and actions.

This is a practice. Stay with it long enough, and it will take you into deeper and richer explorations of the Sacred in you. It isn't always sunshine and blue skies; it can be a wild storm that scours the air and makes way for the oxygen of uncompromising grace.

Notice what happens around you when you become an evolving presence of Divine Order in your home, your family, your community, your places of work and play, of civic life, friendship and worship.

Like calls forth like. We each have the quality of Divine Order within us, as a seed or potential. When we gather with others who are also devoted to expressing Divine Order, we co-create a powerful energy field that shapes the world around us, energetically, and through inspired, powerful, collaborative action.

Fall on your knees, and offer your heart to the earth.

What is too much to bear alone? What do you long to surrender to a greater wholeness? Offer that.

Offer your dreams and divisions, your pull-aparts and come-togethers, your sweetest hopes and shuddering fears, your wants, needs, lusty desires, your feasts and famines.

Offer your refusals, and all that refuses you. Offer your sorrow, your exquisite joy. Offer what cannot be given. Offer the iron that cannot receive.

Offer the fire of the world's suffering, the rain of your tears, the whisper of magic, the hymn and hum of returning tides.

Offer it all.

Feel the cell that is your body vibrating deep in the body of the earth, nourished, breathed, enfolded. At home. Infinitely loved.

Rise up onto your feet. Bring the gift of yourself, renewed, and offer it with both hands to your world.

Each moment of the day, feel and express your profound appreciation, love and gratitude for everything and everyone you encounter.

Be specific with your appreciation. Feel your whole body fill with love and gratitude as you name what you're grateful for.

Here's an example, from my own life, this morning. It may be a bit over the top for you, but I love my shower, and have been known to sing its praises extravagantly, and mostly on-key. :-)

O beautiful flow of hot running water, O magnificent shower, thank you for travelling all the way from the sky to fall as rain and snow on this land. Thank you for making your way through springs, streams, rivers, underground pipes, into my home. Thank you for heating up and softening my scalp and throat, my face, these aching shoulders, and happy arms. Thank you for releasing the tension in my back, for softening my belly, for opening wide the pores of my skin. Thank you for cleansing and washing away all that no longer belongs with me... Thank you, thank you!

Take a moment to fully receive the response from whatever or whoever you're praising, celebrating and appreciating. A shower doesn't have the same consciousness as you or I, but it is sentient, and expressive, and responds to love and appreciation as all beings do.

Do this practice as briefly or as fully as you wish, throughout the day.

Notice how you fill up with love, with appreciation, with gratitude. Notice what happens, in your body, your mind, your heart. How do you feel, at the end of a day of full-on appreciation for all the things, people and situations that inhabit your life?

❋

Consider a situation in which you feel helpless to alter the outcome. One which you've done everything in your power to create, transform, heal, or resolve. One which deflates your illusions of control.

An inner pattern that undermines the trajectory of your soul. A relationship whose hearth-fire has vanished in smoke; a change in the marketplace that's laid your business low and threatens your financial survival; a traumatic event that's upended your life and brought changes you can neither predict nor control. The death or crippling illness of someone you love. Changes in the political, economic or cultural landscape that threaten the foundations of your world. The loss of a dream, the dissolution of life as you've known it, as you'd expected and trusted it would unfold.

Feel your feelings. Feel all of your feelings, for as long as it takes. Hold yourself in your own infinitely tender arms, in your own compassionate, loving heart. Cradle your grief, your lost, abandoned, angry, fearful, sorrowing, broken-hearted selves. Rock yourself, comfort yourself, bring yourself back to the safety and shelter of your soul's presence, of the love that never falters or fails.

When you're ready, gather your strength and courage. Draw them from the four corners of your being, from the earth and sky of you. Fill your heart and belly, your skin and bones, your hands and feet, with the lion of your soul.

Place the situation – the hopeless situation – on the altar of your heart. Invite the spirit of Divine Order to enter, to infuse the situation and its entire ecology with the pattern of its true nature, to transform its congealed intransigence into shimmering molecules of fluid, precisely patterned light.

You cannot control the outcome of this process, any more than you could its earlier incarnations. But the situation, and your relationship with it, will be infused with the grace of Divine Order, healed into life, death, redemption or completion.

Whatever the situation, however excruciating the pain or loss it has brought you, in the light of Divine Order it will become your art.

Judgment is not discernment. It may give you a temporary feeling of power and satisfaction, but it's often just a poor substitute for your soul.

When you find yourself judging – people, situations, yourself, the state of the world, what-is – tune into the helplessness, fear, sadness, anger or emptiness that pools beneath the armour of judgement.

Breathe into these feelings, welcome them into your heart. Make room for them to flow freely, to share their wisdom and truth with you. The light they shine will reveal to you your profound, holy hunger for your soul.

Turn to face and embrace your soul. As you blend with it, surrender to it your longing, your tender, lonely heart, your yearning for communion, love, union, redemption.

Invite your soul to flow through the back of your heart to fill your spine with its radiance. Invite it to infuse and enliven every cell of your body. Welcome its blaze through the layers of your energy body and into your miraculous life.

Feel the vibrancy of your soul made flesh in you.

Fill up with soul food. Let your breath soften, deepen. Rest in the feeling of home, of belonging – with your soul, your body, your world. Re-united with the source of your life, the wellspring of your joy, feel yourself one with everyone and everything – while remaining uniquely, irreplaceably yourself.

Feel the simplicity and love that you are, welcoming your world with open arms, and a discerning, generous heart.

Notice: Where did judgement go?

Make a list of everything that you do entirely by yourself – with no help from anyone or anything else.

Ready? Go.

Nada?

Now, make a list of everything you've done in the past hour. Leave lots of space between each item on your list.

Fill in the spaces with the names of everything and everyone who made it possible for you do what you did.

Finally, make a list of everyone and everything whose lives have been touched in some way by the things you did in the past hour.

What do you know now about yourself, your relationship with life, and your place in the world?

❋

When you're facing a situation whose bleak edges scrape you raw, when doubt, anxiety, lethargy, hopelessness, or despair assail you, deepen your breath, all the way into your belly.

Breathe and soften your joints, your elbows and shoulders, hips, knees, ankles, wrists. Let your brain rest gently in the nest of your skull. Let the inner corners of your eyes lengthen towards the bridge your nose. Lie down on a bed of grass, or in your own sweet bed. Let gravity cradle your spine. Let the palms of your hands and the soles of your feet soften and widen.

Feel your heart pumping blood steadily through your body. Feel your heart expanding to embrace and hold all of you – make room for, and welcome your joy. Now, choose how you want to feel, and act to change your energy accordingly.

Listen to music that enlivens and uplifts you. Explore pieces you've loved in the past, but perhaps haven't listened to in a long while. Really listen, letting the music flow into and transform your cells, reverberate through the chambers of your bones.

Head outdoors. Let sun and wind play with and through you. Let them restore you to your senses. Find a friend to laugh with, to share a meal with. Savour a bowl of nourishing soup. Walk or run by the sea and feel your own wings slipstream you into the raucous world of gulls and cormorants.

Not every situation can be resolved quickly and easily. But you can transform your inner landscape almost instantly. When you do, your most creative, joyful, powerfully generative self will dance with whatever situation you're facing, and find a way to bring it to a state of greater wholeness, clarity and peace.

Build a kiln within your heart. Place in it the wobbly clay shaped by your hands, readying it for the fire that will transform it into an object both beautiful and useful.

Breathe the breath of life into your creation. Fill it with your prayers and blessings for safe passage through the kiln's heat.

Stoke and tend the fire that will harden truth into the forms of beauty, of humble service.

Be patient with the kiln's alchemy. Do not open its doors before the fire has done its work. Revelation has its own timing.

Give yourself permission to be. Rest deeply. Follow your true desires. Play. Savour the beauty of your life, and the tenderness of your world.

If you feel moved to act, let whatever you do be easy, light, playful. No-one to please. Nothing to be responsible for, except your own true desires. You've done enough.

You are a miracle. This is a true story.

Move through today carrying this knowledge in your body and your bones – you are a miracle. Every molecule of your body is a miracle. Every breath you take is a miracle.

Pick a word – any word. Explore it with a receptive heart and enquiring mind today. Remember, you are a guest in its world. Meet it with gratitude for its hospitality, and a sincere desire to get to know it – its heart and mind, its customs and culture.

Each word is a world, containing nations, languages, cultures, genders, life-forms, experiences, world-views that lend it a wide variety of colours, shapes, textures and resonances. It contains its own history, anthropology and archeology, layers of orthodoxy, heterodoxy, adolescent rebellion, adventurous peaks, low-lying valleys.

A word like "pioneer" or "immigrant" or "refugee" holds a multitude of meanings. It comes freighted with the story of migrating generations, shifting national identities, movements of populations both human and animal, exploration, discovery, displacement, pain endured and inflicted, frontiers breached, boundaries drawn and redrawn.

Begin with an invocation and prayer to the soul of the word you've chosen to explore. Ask it, humbly, to allow you into its world, to let you participate in its essence. It is in you, and you in it, but it has its own life, its own singular integrity.

Work outward from there, to understand all that has accrued to it, like nacre wrapped around a grain of sand. Draw on etymological dictionaries, geographical and geological maps of its world, the direct revelations it offers you, and more.

Explore it with your senses. Get to know its tastes and smells, its sounds and textures, its dawn-light and starry midnights. Woo it with poetry, with art, with the gifts you can offer that mirror and express your experience of it.

Each word-world leads you into unknown terrain. Each word reveals both its own mystery, and yours.

Take notes on what you've discovered, by the end of the day. What will you do with these discoveries?

❊

Tune into the subatomic fire that fuels your body, that burns with a nuclear radiance in every cell. Then, tune into the radiance of the creative project that's closest to your heart.

Hold a space of open attentiveness as they commune together – fire with fire, radiance with radiance. Fire's speech is alchemy, transmutation, reduction, dissolution, liberation, transformation.

As they act on each other, and act together, what emerges? What does their communion inspire or clarify for you? What pathway reveals itself?

Map out what you know of this path – quick, without too much thought. What steps need to be taken, in what order, by whom, and by when? Write them down.

Invite the twin fires to draw into their light those allies and resources that will help fulfill their joint purpose. Take the first step that's yours to take, today, now.

Consider your relationship with one of your own creations – something that emerged from your heart, from your delight, from your artistry, from your desire to create, serve, bless, play, explore, nurture and more.

You loved it madly, at one time. At one time, you adored it, you couldn't get enough of it. For days, weeks, months, you stayed up way past your bedtime, canoodling with it, crafting its shape and form. You woke up early, eager to embrace it after a night in which it shimmered through your dreams, a bright current of golden possibility.

You brought it to life, to miraculous, magnificent life. And it renewed your life, in turn. It returned you to your joy, incarnated aspects of your soul you'd never met before. It poured its gifts into the world – truth, radiance, love, nourishment, a safe space to play and grow in wisdom and understanding, a creative container, a garden.

And then...its face grew tiresomely familiar over the breakfast table.

It had needs. It wanted to talk at length about everything, be unbearably intimate. It wanted to hold and be held, to kiss you until your heart liquified into a fine broth, all communion and love. It wanted you to live in that place – that utterly dangerous place. Fearsome in its depth, its openness, its singular devotion to soul, no matter the cost.

So you turned away from it, this creation of your heart. Left it to its own devices while you found new companions to party with.

You find it hard to sleep, these days. Your mind is restless, your heart a distant rumour, a story whose voice it hurts too much to recall.

So, when someone asks you, "If your heart isn't in it, why don't you walk away?" you cannot answer. You hear your heart weeping in a corner of the garden, where it has lived since you banished it. You hear your creation breathing quietly nearby, waiting patiently for your return.

What will you do next? What will you choose?

Your thoughts and beliefs are powerful. They shape your own world, and they shape the world around you.

When you see people and situations as they are, as perfectly unique expressions of the Sacred, when you see their genius and brilliance, their beauty and the immense light of their souls – even when they are at their most vulnerable – your vision contributes to their wholeness. It reminds them of who they truly are. It brings them back to the heart of their belonging.

And the world becomes kinder, more radiant, more forgiving, more welcoming, as more of us remember our true nature.

On the other hand, when you see people, places, things, and situations through the scrim of your own judgments and projections, fears and nightmares – through the distorting lens of your own disconnection – you exert a pressure on their energy fields that adds to the disconnection and suffering of our world and all who dwell here.

You don't have to say unkind or disembowelling words to have this effect – your thoughts become visible even when they remain unspoken. People feel diminished in the presence of judgment and condescension, even if they don't know why.

Choose wisely, because the energy you bring to your world also shapes your inner topography. Meanness, arrogance, create a toxic environment within you as well as around you. You have the power to create heaven or hell through the energy you carry and project.

Use your discernment, to choose those relationships that are wholesome and nourishing. Say a loving but firm No to those that are toxic or simply not right for you. Love includes sovereignty, and clear boundaries. Discernment is a soul quality – and is different from judgment. Trust yourself to know the difference, and to act accordingly.

When you choose to be an agent of wholeness, you become responsible for the energy you bring to any situation. Do your inner work, so you can be a carrier of peace, love, generosity, blessing, and joy. Both you and our world will benefit in profound ways, when you clean up your thoughts and your inner landscape.

❊

If the consequences of a decision are primarily or unequally borne by you, then you have the sovereign right and responsibility to participate fully in making that decision.

Colonialism and other forms of governance that rely on non-participatory decision-making invariably place the decision-making power in one set of hands, and the consequences of those decisions on the backs of another.

Notice where, in your life or the life of your business, you're (primarily or non-reciprocally) bearing the consequences of decisions you've had little or no part in making.

How do you feel about this? What actions will you take to assert your sovereignty in these situations?

Notice where, in your life or the life of your business, you're making decisions whose consequences are asymmetrically borne by others. What actions will you take to honour their sovereignty in these situations, and invite their participation in the decision-making process?

Make sheltering branches of your arms, deep-shaded canopy in your belly, a sun-filled meadow of your heart. The wren of Grace alights wherever she's offered loving hospitality.

Which beam of sunlight is yours? Which breeze, which air current, which drop of rain belongs to you?

Can you identify it? Register a deed of ownership? Lock up or punish those on whom it bestows itself, unbidden?

What beliefs do you hold about other kinds of ownership that are equally untenable? How do they affect your happiness? Your relationship with your world?

Next, consider what's yours because it belongs with you, and you with it. Because your mutual love and tenderness, devotion and delight braid you together like the entwined limbs of a great tree.

What do you know, in your heart, about right relationship withownership? What do you know about right relationship with belonging? What will you do with this knowledge?

Dislodge that one crucial boulder in the stream, and the power you liberate will sweep away all lesser obstacles, opening the way for unobstructed creation.

❋

Take your eyes off the prize long enough to see the treasure beneath your feet.

Pain speaks. Its voice may be too loud, fearfully frantic, too hoarse for you to easily discern what it is trying to say.

Meet it with an open heart, offer it your love, kindness and full attention, and it will whisper to you its quiet truth.

Healing lies in the heart of your relationship with pain.

Today, be the yeast that makes everything rise.

Imagine a world – our world – in which there are no women. Not a world in which women have been made extinct, but one in which women never existed.

Imagine.

What would be missing, in a world devoid of women? How would life evolve? How would our species reproduce? What other life-forms would disappear from our world, in the absence of women?

Who or what would embody the qualities and functions of women?

Where would all the feelings, needs and desires land? The ones that are currently projected onto women? Who would take responsibility for them?

Draw a panoramic view that includes the gaps, the consequential alterations in human evolution and history, as a result of evolution without women.

Now imagine that you are one of the architects of the human species. What would you weave into the holes in the web of the world left by the absence of women?

Become the thread that's woven into one of those holes today.

You hold in your hand an invitation to the Great Cosmic Birth Feast. It's inscribed in love, written on the vellum of truth: You are invited to participate in the Earth's evolution. To build a relationship with power that is inclusive, generative, and benefits all beings, including the planetary being we call Earth.

You are being called to learn from the history of our species, to forego paradigms of dominance and submission, exploitation, abuse, divisiveness, and power-over, in whatever forms they show up in your life.

You are invited to take your place as a generative partner in the ecology of being. To place the creative power of your human incarnation in service to the earth and to all beings who live here. To offer your hands and heart to help shape the evolving energy body of the earth.

You are the host, not the guest, at this birth-feast. You are a creator, not simply a consumer, of the earth's bounty. You are invited to end humanity's brutal legacy of pain, of arrogant exploitation. You are invited to transform the story of humanity as pillagers and profiteers. You are invited to become a loving steward of our planetary home, to nurture and preserve the miracle of life on earth for all beings.

Attune to the process of planetary evolution. Attune to the invitation it offers you, to become one of the great ancestors of the world of tomorrow.

How does it feel to stand in this place, holding this invitation in your hand? Joyous, exciting? Terrifying? Overwhelming? Liberating? Or something else entirely?

Begin by embracing your own humanity. Meet yourself where you are. Wrap the invitation around your heart. Be curious, loving, playful, generous with yourself.

Who are you, beyond the roles that define you?

What light and power do you hold that's uniquely yours, that is the blaze of your incarnation?

How will you meet this invitation to host the party? To be a creative, generative source of love and power in the earth's evolution and rebirth?

What can you, and only you, bring to the Great Cosmic Birth Feast?

Wave goodbye to dramatic agendas. This moment holds the whole nourishing, blessed, miraculous world in the palm of its hand.

❖

Enter the mouth of a galaxy. On your belly, navel gliding along the shimmering spiral of its undulant tongue. Float in on the bellows of its breath, the galaxy breathing you in, the galaxy breathing.

Swim among the stars, your body turning over and over in rivers of radiance.

Who are you, afloat in the spaces between stars? What keeps you from colliding into their gravitational fields?

Be that, today.

❊

Hold our world, with all its sorrow, joy, pain, violence, tenderness and beauty in the flow of Divine Grace. Be an anchor point for grace to do its work of healing and restoration.

Too can be a bridge, or the sound of a slammed door.

You belong too. I love music too. We are here too.

You are too much. I am too slow. Too little too late.

The words you use become you, and become your world. What shape does your too take?

Choose the too you want to be. Choose the too you want to bring into the world. Then be that too. Do that too.

Power is the active form of love. It's a quality of soul, so it's already within you, as a seed or potential. You can cultivate it, expand your capacity to embody and express it, and use it to help shape the world in which you want to live.

Sometimes, when you feel most powerless, events occur that remind you: you have the power to choose. You can choose the stories that are yours to live. You can step out of the stories that don't belong to you; and step into the ones that do.

You can shape the stories of your future by swimming out of the current of your past, and into a new story that's held in the creative Flow of the Universe.

You do this by loving and trusting your choices; by keeping your word; by living in harmony with your deepest values; by honoring your vision; by listening to, and acting upon, the promptings of your imagination and your heart.

You make friends with your stories, the ones that you've forgotten, the ones you've ignored, neglected, left to languish, untended – and the ones you've embraced, loved, welcomed into your life.

You make friends with yourself, your world, your great, shining soul.

When you do, you liberate not only your own soul's power, but you collaborate with the powers of wholeness to shape a world of freedom, prosperity, love, divine order, justice and fulfillment for all beings.

Here are some questions about power and powerlessness to explore, if you wish:

To whom, or to what, have you given your power away? Who or what has the power to "make" you feel bad (e.g. Money? Traffic? Time? Words? Health? Your ex? Your social media feed? Systems of governance? Natural disasters?)

What patterns of power and powerlessness have you inherited? What patterns of power and powerlessness do you participate in? What role do you play in perpetuating these patterns?

What stories do you tell about power? Are they true? To whom do those stories belong?

Choose. Choose how you relate to power. Choose a more coherent story. Then, act to bring your new story to life.

Barnacle: A sessile, parasitic crustacean with no true heart.

Where, in your body, in your life, do you host barnacles?
What happens when you liberate yourself from their grip?

How to create your heart's desires:

Love your creative self. Love the joy you feel when you create. Love the way your creation weaves you into the warp and woof of the world.

Love your creation. Love its shining horizon, its muddy middle, its blobby, babbling, baby beginning.

Love your world so much, you'll offer it your art & heart. Even when its scary.

Do your work. Every day. Do it with joy, with tears, with the whole delicious, quivering, rocketing mess and muddle and masterfulness of you.

Gather your friends and allies. Let many hands and hearts hold you.

Create! You'll never know who you'll become, until you do.

ACKNOWLEDGEMENTS

Deep bow of gratitude to: Richard Miller, for impeccable artistry in designing this book. Mandy McIlwraith and Amber Kinney, for wrangling the project into shape so beautifully. Beloved friends, Danielle LaPorte, Jen Louden, Judith Snider, Andrea J. Lee for loving support, creative play, and being sources of infinite delight. My family, friends, clients and students for your presence, constancy, and devotion to being the activity of soul, making our world a kinder, more generous place.

HIRO BOGA

Hiro Boga, MFA, is a writer, teacher, business strategist, and mentor to creative leaders who are shaping a world that works for everyone. She is a pioneer in the field of soul-powered creativity and leadership.

Hiro writes and teaches at the frontier where soul and subtle energy meet artistic integrity, creative freedom, and renewable prosperity in service to a world of wholeness, peace, and provision for everyone.

For close to forty years, she has guided thousands of clients and students through adventures in creative consciousness that result in practical ways to build a better, more beautiful world.

Read more, and enjoy a wealth of free resources, including online Deva Cards, at HiroBoga.com. You can also connect with her on Facebook and Instagram, where she shares daily insights, stories, inspiration and more to accompany you on your journey.

- hiroboga.com
- hiroboga.com/deva-cards
- facebook.com/hiroboga.inc
- instagram.com/hiroboga

Made in the USA
San Bernardino, CA
14 December 2019

61473635R00102